Mockingbird's Proverbs

"What an astonishing and breathtaking book this is—the brilliance of the poems' aphoristic nonchalance and their biting wisdoms move like large uncut diamonds on a roulette wheel. There is no description for this whiplash tenderness piercing all of these poems."

—David St. John, author of *Prayer for My Daughter*

"Gail Wronsky has been at it for a long time. At what? Well, poetry, for one, but even before poetry, I imagine, a surrealist drive, by which I mean keeping tabs on death as filtered through an icy, blue-lipped, Kodacolor, apocalyptic, consciousness. Even her torrential proverbs are surreal, and her confessionalism hallucinates, with its memories of music boxes shaped like French cathedrals, its erotic marigolds. 'Death ferments deep in the wrinkles of certain trench coats,' she writes. It inhabits every space in these poems, the air that shrouds commas, the aperture that opens where the line breaks like a bone. *Mockingbird's Proverbs* is, at its core, an act of mystic generosity. When mystics convey visions, it is holy instruction. It's dowry, legacy. *Be subversive*, Wronsky's poems tell us, *while you still can.* The imagination has always represented a defiance of the suburban lawn, a revolt against tyranny. Ask Lorca, a member of Wronsky's lineage. Ask the mockingbird, with its downcast eye".

—Diane Seuss, author of *Modern Poetry* and *frank: sonnets*

"Wronsky takes us to the existential theatres of a life lived to its fullest, or is it its emptiest? 'Or maybe it's the light/pouring in like eggnog, or the/deep eroticism of marigolds.' Only a poet who has dived into the wreck can extract wisdom with such singular West Coast wit. Family, love and memory are transformed in an 'eternal spiral notebook' overflowing with grit and compassion. *Mockingbird's Proverbs* are poems in conversation with our troubled age, with the revelations of time and the mysteries of death. Poignancy skirts the borders of irony, and humor is never far behind their philosophical depths. 'Exuberance is Beauty,' William Blake proclaimed in his 'Proverbs of Hell.' Wronsky's poems continue that exuberance."

—Ramón García, author of *The Chronicles*

Also by Gail Wronsky

Poetry

Born in a Barn on Venus (with artwork by Gronk)
The Stranger You Are (with artwork by Gronk)
Under the Capsized Boat We Fly: New & Selected Poems
Imperfect Pastorals
So Quick Bright Things
Poems for Infidels
Dying for Beauty
Again the Gemini are in the Orchard

Chapbooks

Some Disenfranchised Evening
Blue Shadow Behind Everything Dazzling
Dogland

Translations

Fuegos Florales (Flowering Fires) by Alicia Partnoy
Volando Bajito (Little Low Flying) by Alicia Partnoy

Coauthored Books

Tomorrow You'll Be One of Us (with Chuck Rosenthal and Gronk)
The Shortest Farewells are the Best (with Chuck Rosenthal)
Bling & Fringe (with Molly Bendall)
A Giant Claw (with Gronk)

Poetry for Children

The Moose in the Moon

Mockingbird's Proverbs

Gail Wronsky

WHITE PINE PRESS | BUFFALO, NEW YORK

White Pine Press
P.O. Box 236
Buffalo, NY 14201
www.whitepine.org

Publication of this book was supported by public funds from the New York State Council on the Arts, with the support of Governor Kathy Hochul and the New York State Legislature, a State Agency.

Acknowledgements: See page 78.

Printed and bound in the United States of America.

ISBN 978-1-945680- 82-3

Library of Congress Control Number: 2024939694

Contents

In Spite of Everything

Mockingbird's Proverbs

For the Surrealists

Listen to the mockingbird, listen to the mockingbird.
The mockingbird is singing o'er her grave
Listen to the mockingbird, listen to the mockingbird,
Still singing where the weeping willows wave.

Traditional song

Out of the cradle endlessly rocking,
Out of the mocking-bird's throat, the musical shuttle . . .

Walt Whitman

Mockingbird's Proverbs

Proverbs #1

We're a stone's throw
from eternity. We know that because the sky is filled
with unfinished frescoes and spiral staircases, because
there are trap doors in certain poems. The day will turn
emptiness into dark masses of sleep, which is a kind of
dense lava enveloping each city at night, which is also a
patchwork quilt of the shadows left behind by forgotten ghosts.
Diary entries found in the nightstands of our grandmothers
contain unexpected apathies and understandable rage. If gods
do dream, no dream goes to waste. Live your life under
the sign of pearls, or the sign of secrets. Wait until everyone
has left then look at yourself in the mirror and begin.
It's possible to move on without moving.

Proverbs #2

When you write,
lay down the text torrentially. That agreeable friction,
the light granulation of the paper under the lead of your
pencil, is God. Commas are possessed by shamans. The
space you take up in this sliver of the continuum cannot
be filled with blueberries or bread. This will all pass,
it will. Take a long, cool sip of sorrow and doubt that
sorrow exists. Walk into the shadows painted on your
hand. The dreams of yesterday are lies, you know that.
If you meet the person lighting up the room, the person
whose eyes are the color you imagine desire to be, go to
bed with them. In the morning, if you don't recognize the
alien body lying there, ask it nicely to leave.

Proverbs #3

There's nowhere to go.
There isn't. In this world, everything alludes to
everything else. You're not as bad as you think
you are. You're not as bad as pain. Three words
you never want to use in a poem: *cheeks, sapphire,*
cacophony. Don't think your flaws and disguises
make you unique. The woman in the rhinoceros mask
is a god. If you care at all about the complexities of
beauty, act as if this were not a big deal. No one
will suspect you of giving a shit. Pretend to be
anesthetized, especially on clear, silent nights.
Itches are always the same. That's true of boredom
and suffocation—always the same. The deepest sleep
is the sleep of whomever is dreaming us. When you
are lonely, each cell of your body aches with loneliness.
Having a good attitude takes the good right out of
you. Don't blame the dead for your grief.

Proverbs #4

Sometimes it gets really late
really early. Time to brush away the noisy flocks of demons that possess you and imagine yourself shining the way an insect shines—brightly, almost phosphorescently—in a lamp. Imagine yourself that tiny and beautiful. Imagine singing a wispy song like a mosquito. Imagine that Time, which doesn't exist, is God. That love is a place to hide safely for a moment—that thatched cottage by the Yellow River. That there's no more stupid shit you have to remember. Days pass, each one turning unreadable pages. Poetry happens when the body speaks out of the thick darkness of its imagery. What we call the past is simply the way things happened to be arranged once. I will always be the one singing the anthem of the Infinite in a bargain basement.

Proverbs #5

Never use *amid, licking,* or *shiver*
in a poem. Never disrupt the glittering gray scales of river water with your mind. What I know is this: you have a reader waiting anxiously for your poetry. It's me. Though some days I feel as though I can't let another person into my brain. A good hat is one that makes you look as though your hair is on fire. As though your eyes express the insane delight and speed of life. When is a cypress tree smaller than an orange? This is what I say when I don't know what to say. Write it when you don't know what to write. Making art makes you fold in on yourself almost to the point of pain. The silences of others, when translated, contain testimony spoken by the exhausted or by the dead and for the dead. Serenity is transmittable, kind of the way diseases are. Always carry a knife disguised as a pencil. Always.

Proverbs #6

Don't search for sand
through sand. Just don't. Don't try to write a final, definitive record of who you've been—it would read like a funeral guestbook, and, really, are any one of us one of those aristocratic writers who will have guestbooks, who will have funerals? Only the immortals, who are immaterial, can afford not to care about material things. Gather in your hands the metal debris, the black powder that no broom eliminates, the leaves of grass to which you've given names, the pieces of cloth that listen to you. I never wanted to pass as someone exemplary. Like Fernando Pessoa I have more than one soul. So do you. One of mine is shaped like an hourglass. I'll leave it behind me when I die, hoping that someone turns it over.

Proverbs #7

We scribble poems
and political speeches in the same eternal spiral notebook. Some of us carry absurd, childishly forged fake passports. Some of us aren't going to make it in New York or anywhere. Dreams distill their pleasures like icicles, drop by drop. Still, they rarely quench our thirst for the fantastic. Let your eyes sweep the space that glitters just in front of your shoes for that. I get this now: sometimes complexity is just stupid. Try not to be crushed by the night's loud waves of black lava. The truth is most people's lives are crushed into servitude. Death ferments deep in the wrinkles of certain trench coats. I'm trying to cross the boundary between art and all other forms of communication here. Sometimes the future is latent in us without our knowing it. Perhaps you could leave your contact information.

Proverbs #8

The forgotten ones die;
the ones doing the forgetting die too. In the meantime, bathe in the wine-drunk twilight of now. When death sounds its horn, when you're forced to kiss the cold body in the casket, believe that whatever can heal in us will. It's the only illusion left to me. Shun paradise, shun rewards, shun glory. Listen to the gnawing of the termites. You know they're there. People whose lives are lived by viewless windows pull the shades down when they hear the supernatural noises of the night rolling off mountains, awakening echoes in shadowy caves, hurling out into the darkness a thousand tragic sounds. I do too. Tears as big as fists fall as hard as fists on the table. If you swallow one, it will seem as if a perfect circle had closed. As if death did not exist. Ever. Now, what are we going to do to keep the capitalists from pissing all over our moon?

Proverbs #9

Eternity is in love
with the productions of time, says Blake. Sit here with me, in the
time we have, so that eternity can love us. I'll admit, at times like
these it's hard to love the sapphire fluids hardening in our bones.
Or to say "eternity" while looking at the mirror—the mirror you've
glowered at, fought with, fucked in front of. The mirror in which
you look like a trout, your house and all its cacophonous apathy
behind you. Condemn the hell that is prison, not the person who is
prisoner. Hell is ok, were it not for the god-awful screaming, says
the evil one. Poems are written on the arthritic spines of writers
who came before us. Future poets will write their poems on ours.
(Will it hurt? Yes, probably.) Paint your face the way you want to
paint it and wear it out into the world. Making art is both cheeky
and holy. You can't run away forever. Run away anyway.

Proverbs #10

What now, when nothing
counts anymore. When God is dangling the fire threat again.
When people think of kicking you in your tomb. We need to imag-
ine cataracts of mercy. We need to imagine a way out of here. We
need to stand on the crumbling, invisible feet of the past. Not a
feather adorns us, yet we furrow on. Hadn't we been stark raving
something on Tuesday? Today we linger at the border of our
knowledge. We want to know more. But knowledge is illusive—it
dissolves like a wave before materializing again in a slightly
different form, darkened by clouds of interpretation, or by clouds
formed out of the nosy questions of the unbelievers. Replace the
hideousness of current events with your own absurd images. With
your poem for vocal trio and orchestra. Learn to read the lips of
ghosts.

Proverbs #11

We victimize the world
that victimizes us. We live inside ourselves as if we were dreaming a dream that had no beginning and no end, a dream about nothing, a dream composed of clouds that drift silently past, covering a sky we have long since forgotten. What to do? Replace the oar in your hand with a bird. Love the blood filigree lacing your eyes. You've earned it. All around us spreads a desert and there's no one here to tell us "This is the way." Righteousness needs to be proven wrong. When what you said was dark turns out to be light, forgive yourself. Days bristle with potential booby traps, which is why we sometimes feel like actors in a gangster movie, abandoned by the scriptwriter in some sinister parking garage. Danger as easy to come by as a fix.

Proverbs #12

Poetry doesn't die.
It will be there in the afterlife. As blatantly plangent, painful and piercing as any *fado* that ever emerged from a throat. We need it now the way a shipwrecked man needs a plank of wood to hold on to, the way a seed needs sun. So our brains attach themselves to words, go over and over the same thoughts, plunge into them, drown in them, phrases that lead us along vertiginous paths into deep valleys from which arise murmurs of voices that seem to be calling us. Voices that can help us feel in our flesh the wound that makes us human. In other words, poetry. Poetry, which is a bit like the milkweed pod I pulled open one summer in my hand. Fine white strands of silk with brown seeds attached floated up into still air. When I grabbed them, they clung to my skin, making my hands seem strange to me—almost supernaturally beautiful. And made the wild wilderness of my youth rise up around me, even wilder.

A Portion of Shadow

Both of my hands are frightened

Maybe it's the fine dancing dust
of the air today that makes me
realize I've been writing on the
wavy surface of the wind all my
life. Or maybe it's the light
pouring in like eggnog, or the
deep eroticism of marigolds. I've
always felt that my soul must be
made of infrared silk embroidered in
threads of mercury, and if only I could
read the story written there,
I'd know my past and my future.
My toenails are as shiny as ten black
beetles. I'm afraid my imagination
has shrunk down small enough to fit in
a demi-tasse spoon, but just once I'd like
to conjure up an ocean or a waterfall

of solid marble. Your body curls
like a shrimp on my sheepskin rug.
Sometimes the blue of the sky comes
deep inside me and hollows me out.
Sometimes I leave my house and when
I come back the people I left there have
changed in ways I can't explain. I live
here now where pronouns have a
conditional tense. Today I think I'd
like to engage in ordinary conversation—
like what you'd have in a hair salon.
English would be perfectly ok for this.
So would lorikeet language. When I
opened the jeweled box you gave me,
Death, once so far away, came barreling
toward me. I lay there, pitiful as a skinned
mink, but it hurried by awkwardly,

mumbling like a person trying to bluff their
way through a conversation in a language
they don't understand. There are
images that can't be put into words.
Light needs so much dark in order to
dazzle. Still, I'd like to read your
mother's autobiography. And I'd like
to help you write your own so that you
can escape from both of them. You,
who remind me so much of a motorcycle
burning fearlessness as its fuel. Have you
noticed how that ruddy gray hen of a
cloud lays the setting sun into a bed
of incandescence on the horizon tonight?

I have become imaginary too

Haunted by the green steam rising off these hills, I look to where you are not and silently agree with you in your absence that with all the crap being piled on us we'll need explosives to open up any breathing room. These things could change but I doubt it.

And then you return with your nurture, nurture, nurture. Maybe you just need donuts, you say. I say the pounding in my head reminds me of percussion day in preschool. We'll never be grandparents. This isn't jazz we're listening to, it's the extravagances of some conventional romance and nostalgia.

And this is the part of the song that makes me think the dishwasher's running. Somedays we're just skittish. Somedays we believe that God is pain. And therefore heaven is one heartache after another. Antony and Cleopatra are characters in Shakespeare.

We're not. You say all this has been said before. Well, fuck me, I'm a crazy old person. I smell like iron or salad. I've slept in the bed of my ghost. And back to the green steam of the beginning: *Verde, te quiero verde.*

We're one inch from hell and I'm exploring the confessional mode

I want to drink summer's warm,
green blood. I want to inhale air
that is full of hashish
and whimsy. I want to lie down
with the puppets of my childhood
in their dusty
crates.

I want to believe that evening
is a blind alley of aromas
into which the world rushes once a day. I
want to believe that among
the verses of certain poets swallows fly out
in great numbers.

I confess, there is someone who
accompanies me
like a breath, like
a flip side, like an accomplice
in an eternal dialogue. They
accuse me of bluffing, of deliberate
mystification. Not even I

know who they are— a guardian angel?
some inner critic? But let's not talk
about that now. I'll panic
like an amateur wheeler-dealer
who's on the losing end of a
life-and-death transaction.

Let the complicated times roll

for my mother, who has schizophrenia

We've been lost for so
long in mysticism—

fighting madness with the
slender blade

of lucidity, feeling the steel
needles of panic, emerging

from forests of outrageous
laughter or

marooned on an island of absurdity.
Sometimes I think that sanity lounges

on a tree branch right above
us, like a puma, but we are

only allowed to see the tip of its
tail. Who knows

what trees
dream of, she asks. I dream of

the fear I have of myself.
And of her. It's something

about the blending of
tenderness and cruelty around

her mouth. Although I love her,
it makes my soul shudder.

Your brain is made of glass

for Gronk

Mine is full of tiny hummingbirds with silk-thin wings.
Why are we friends? It could be because my left arm
is made of glass too, or because when we walk about
in sneakers over asphalt, we both feel the ghosts of the
underworld teasing the soles of our feet. Some days
you gleam under art gallery lights as if you were wearing
the reflected shimmering of your admirers' whisperings.
Other days your thoughts are as unknowable as the Martian
ice fields on which pure white alien insects dream their lives.

A friend asked me about my childhood

for Theresia

I remember night creaking under the pressure of parents sleeping,
the thick lava of their breathing, and all the doors, the garages,
the fireplaces in which wind whined.

I remember the many doomed patches of suburban lawn we
inhabited, and vast skies filled with telephone poles, drying linens,
and imaginary people ascending into heaven.

At times a fire broke out in a distant neighborhood.

At times the moon seemed to be made of brass, or it resembled an
abalone shell, or a fish scale.

I remember waving butterfly nets in a night sky full of spirits,
catching nothing but believing fully that no one's soul should be
allowed to escape.

There was a music box shaped like a French cathedral. It spun
around when you wound it with a key, opening like angel wings
many tiny stained-glass windows.

I remember that cows, lying down, looked to me like burial
mounds. That their eyes were sad. That we ate them.

The chirping of tiny birds

Hmm. It looks   like the sun has entered
again the pensiveness   inside clouds.

Darkness is   swelling; its fantastic
dough is rising.

Amid   vapors of summer torpor
and gin, you   reach your hand

into your pocket and   show me, like a handful
of tiny seashells, the cherished   accumulation

of possibilities roiling around   inside you.
Instantly, we   find ourselves rapt in some

long-ago life, some   distant   pre-existence.
Oh yes,   and now the chirping of tiny birds

pours like thin streams of liquid silver through
a   light netting   of mosquitoes,

stripping the   landscape of any   illusion
it had of its   exteriority.

What's that noise?

When the opium entered our veins, it swelled
them with desire for the unknown.
I wanted to see through the eyes of an octopus.
Now, night's nearing, and there's
an absurd turbulence in the clouds. Nothing
can be heard over the crushing din of heaven.
Not the small sound of someone
dying, which is like the sound of a dropped
screw rolling slowly back and forth on a table.
Or like grains of salt falling on salad leaves.
I've been dreaming of fire on a piece of
paper. I've been dreaming I was a comma,
interrupting the clatter of conversation. A
stone on the road. I have phone booths and
prison cells in my body—hermetic spaces
where whispers of the living and the dead
can sometimes be intercepted.

I try to notice things

God knows, I've been lost for a long time
in thought, contemplating the fears and joys
the soul has of itself—
so I haven't had much time to write in my
noticing notebook. A few nights ago, though,
I had a dream in which I used the word
'visceral' in a poem, so I wrote that down
("use the word 'visceral' in a poem").
"Thanks for that," I said to my dream-self.
"I'm just here to help you live in your body,"
it replied, in a voice that had a kind of
melancholy quivering. It was then that I felt
a dawning of the fear of death. It was then
that my enormous soul rose up from its pit
and held me in its gaze—as if with tusks.

The poet at 17

My youth? It ended the night I totaled the family's
Chevrolet. Days later I was older. By which
I mean that although my bones were fractured my
mind became large. I entered a vivid coma—

my mental state a kind of spooky theater, a seemingly
endless end. I thought perhaps it was heaven. For hours
I existed in a hazy place strewn with ashes of my
memories. Everything was beautiful— lit by light blue—

everything swayed. I remember at some point
a brisk morning breeze blew, a bit acrid, bearing
the smell of herbs. Of holiday cooking. I moved
around in barely protected layers of my own brain,

through sheer veils, beneath cloudy spaces,
there where unease, animal fury and ancestral fears
hide, still unformulated. I had no idea who I was. Nor
where. I knew myself only as an indefinite being,

with language and powers no one else knew about, nor
could know about. When I tried to speak, words clung
to my tongue like down, verbs tangled up with nouns.
I called to the gods who, as usual, weren't in attendance.

Perhaps I'd moved through pain and reached the
shamanic realm of non-life and non-death. Perhaps that
describes what happened to me. The memory shimmers
uneasily in my mind, as if it belonged to someone else's

story, a story on which I have already turned the page. What
can I tell you? Since then, I've lived as a strange inhabitant
of my own body. Unreal stars burst like bubbles inside
me. When I look in the mirror, when I stare into my own

eyes, I can dive in and live other lives there. I can say that the absolute, that otherness, is an oddly tender space. That the brain can be filled with light. And with gray, gray sagebrush rolling windily away.

A vividly pale, panicky light in the sky

a sonnet

Rhetoric annoys me in the end. It reminds me
of Lucky's speech in *Waiting for Godot:*

quaquaquaquaqua God in his white beard qua.
But sometimes I have difficulty chasing the

argument-making impulse from my brain. *Ergo,*
I've been sitting here in eerie sunlight for days,

desiring relief from the machinery of logic, which
is a lot like the machinery of war. I'm thinking

about the profound orphanhood of abandoned cities.
I'm thinking about the sinister nature of political maps,

and about the exquisite idiosyncracy of the blue maps
crossing the narrow plains of our wrists—pulsing

subtly the way that my gods dream in rhythmic
conversation with the universe while they sleep.

Under the influence of a nightmare

We sat as if in the shade of our own fate—

as if on the shore of our fate—

We moved through rooms that did not exist.

We moved as if we were getting ready to

depart for another dimension. We listened

to the secret, creaking life of the floor. This

was nothing unusual, given the familiar tissue

of our nocturnal reveries—those wavy terrains

lined with azure wind—those places thick with

the private glances that mirrors reflect back

to one another. . .

Above us in the ceiling's rafters there were

beaded chandeliers that looked like giant squid.

They moved their long tentacles slowly in

a kind of silent dancing. "I had something else in

mind," you said while kneading the astral dough

between my body and my soul. "I did too," I said,

poking my fingers against the final imprisoning

membrane of your consciousness . . .

I'm no longer eager for danger

Everywhere I rest, I lie on a wound.

And there you are
on a farther shore
wearing a black
coat just like the
one I have on.
You, who

skewered me—
who turned my
thoughts into a
blue stew in my
brain.

Don't even mention the tension
that looms. Or the huge

wildebeest that is love,
the beast now lazily
turning to survey me,
one of the jackals
yapping crazily
at its feet.

The entrails of some roadkill: six unfinished prose poems

1

In the oldest form of prehistoric cave art, a hand is an ideogram signifying "I. This page is my cave. These words my handprints.

2

There were countless dogs barking in the darkness. I was listening to the song *What a Little Moonlight Can Do . . .*

3

"It is not the image, and it is not even the absence of the image," said the teacher.

"Half of my brain is a loaf of bread and half of my brain is a shadow," said the young poet.

4

It was only a small, closed-down factory whose owner had gone bankrupt and then killed himself. It was only the local tv weatherman in a hot air balloon, holding a sign that said, *I'm lonely! Marry me!*

5

"Why don't you describe the fog here that sticks to our skin like a coat of invisible leeches," she said.

6

Like great gray owls, we moved as one with the night.

In what the dead call 'the real world'

We who are alive live in its muck, its dust,

its hard-won hopefulness, even though combat

after combat we lose everything, sometimes

even the floors we walk on and the ghostly winds

whistling beneath them. Some of us go into the

streets daily and air our wounds there. Or we

get locked up the way one locks up harmful animals,

unless we're willing to die in our own extinctions.

It'd be best, the dead say, if we covered our tracks

better or left things the way we found them. Instead

we leave our signatures everywhere—on bodies,

on buildings, on weapons, on poems.

In the general nowness of now

For once I'm not thinking
about death. I'm just
thinking about how to
beautify this page.

But my mind is as
dry as the ocean is
on the wings of a
fly. All I can hear

are the soft rumors of
weeds. They say there
might be scorpions in
the sugar bowl . . .

The sky is the color of the
eyelids of my mother in the
sixties—aquamarine.

She's old now and
afraid of birds,
afraid of the
frenzied void they
leave when they
startle.

I'm afraid of drawing
names and shapes out
of nothing. But you
never know

from which absence
the muse
in her ice blue
halo will
arise.

A night in which we seem to live

Evening—woven of swirling, and of crazy
phantoms, and now this wavering night seems
sheathed in sheets streaked with green satin.
As usual, while I'm busily digesting the rib
bones of the day, you study the mesmerizing
anatomy of your hallucinations. There's always
that one matter that remains unclear, right?
Always one mystery lying there impervious
as a poppy seed. Always that one dream plane
vanishing into sunny nothingness. And
somewhere a curtain opening slightly like lips
that part without knowing they do in our sleep.

I dreamt that my brain invented a new language

and now those
brave new words

have faded,
leaving not

a syllable behind.
And what I'm left with

aches in me—
the possibilities I

dreamt of—poems
that would

let loose all
the complexities of

the heart; stubborn
meanings in the creases

of our souls; verbal
doorways into what is

absolute; metaphors
that would die for us

if they could. Now,
in the old language,

only artifice reveals
itself as truth;

lines of poetry release
abysmal melodies. The

weird theater that is
my brain is filled

only with the insistent
calling of the mockingbird.

In Spite of Everything

We sit as if in a birdcage, delicately

Heck, we feel horrible! Because the grass beneath
our bird feet glistens with some kind of poisonous
glue and we don't dare step on it. Instead, we sit on

our perches patiently—the way shoes sit when human
feet have been removed. Our balcony confesses its
emptiness to a somber sky. In this post-apocalyptic

phantasm of an afternoon we remember dry seed pods
erupting softly—the way grasshoppers used to—and
decades—and sighs. We wait to be rescued by science.

We twitter like Victorian wind-up birds—our beaks
as sharp as opened soup cans. We envy those birds their
jeweled plumage. They envy us because caught

in our ribcages a stubborn vitality endures—its rhythms
as familiar as any remembered lullaby or scar.

The moon is in labor

after the reversal of Roe v. Wade

At least she's pretending to be,
in sisterly solidarity. It's
not a joke, but the whole world's
taking it badly. Meanwhile
I sit here pretending to be a
flame in a thrown bottle.
I pretend that curved horns
grow out of my ears
when I hear of injustices. And
meanwhile like the faint cigar
lights of the darkened lounges
where world leaders fraternize,
the moon's red light glows
then fades. Her labor proves
to be, well, laborious. Mine
was too, although this poem
burst forth from my brain
like a boot or a god: furious.

Watch out: I'm thinking feelingly

and it's only midnight, man. My eyes have the oily sheen of roasted coffee, and I want to know what to do about the fragility of birds; the red radiance of the sea; the clamoring of angels, of animals, of all the dead poets and rock stars? How do I move out of the vestibule of night and enter truer night when there are all these plush, white moths flying around my walls in quiet panic?

The arbitrary as inevitability

The moon forges a shimmering corridor
in a dark sea of thunderous doors.
—Yun Wang

Open one and find yourself
on a beach you went to
on a whim once, long ago—

the beach where he asked you
to dance and howl, naked
around a bonfire—

the beach where you said,
I'd rather die, or
bite me, asshole—

where we sat on the shore
and watched four decades
rush by like smoke.

Elegy for all of us

Over my dead body a veil of luminous
blue moss will grow. That

particular blue will be an old color—
it will look like an ad from the past—like

Kodacolor, or the blue that used to show up
occasionally on the shady side of fern fronds.

It would be startling, if anyone were around
to see it. As startling as yellow,

a color I once sought solace in, rubbing
dandelions under my chin. The other dead

folks here will have faces as white and translucent
as wax. Our mouths will be set slightly off-kilter

into smiles, which is how we all recognized each other
when we were alive—by smiling—how we

knew that we could trust each other with our
lives, which, it turns out, we couldn't.

The play I'm in sucks

It's as dark as *King Lear*, but not as wordy.

I play "an unimportant character in a play
with no audience." *(C'est moi!)*

I do a lot of standing, holding unreadable signs—
directed to "jerk [my] head as if the wind were

pulling [my] hair with invisible fingers."
For the climax, the lead, a handsome poet, says,

"The bones I buried beneath my bedroom window
sing all night." And I deliver my only line:

"Everyone's dead, Adrian, but me."
Then there's the sound of someone walking through

a tunnel in spiked heels, followed by an image of
fire reflected in a person's eyes. The audience

is instructed to blow their black candles out
simultaneously. One reviewer said the final

moments "carry a lot of post-exotic irony."
Doesn't everything?

This isn't death; it's a hair salon

I made my pilgrimage to the palazzo of beauty
where death
is just another mirror. There

in an immense aquarium bald octopi
camouflaged themselves and collided. I said

to my colorist who is a genius (his fingernails
painted in rainbows), *Today I want*
Kim Novak in Vertigo *blonde.* He obliged.

At home, holding a souvenir keychain
shaped, oddly, like the Golden Gate Bridge,
my partner said, *I didn't go to the palace, but*
I, too, have been changed
in inexplicable ways.
I didn't know whether to fear him or applaud.

The house I will die in

I hired a psychic to take me there.

You have no idea, she said as we drove,
the constant pressure to predict, when
oftentimes my thoughts are as opposite as
God and Satan.

Mine too, I said.

We stopped in front of a yellow bungalow.
Is this the place? I asked.

Yes, she said, *in its basement I see*
many small worms busily
spinning white silk for your burial clothes.

Out front a magnificent rose bush was getting
mouth-to-mouth resuscitation from the wind.

I want to be buried in fuchsia, I said.

They're making a movie of my movie, or, you just can't control these things!

My movie, *Panic of the Arabesques*, was a

super low-budget Super-8 thing I made

in college. It took on issues like the tragedy

of sunflowers, like what would happen if

femaleness was deprived of brakes. It tried

hard in its way to express the inexpressible

adequacy of this splendid project, life—

full of piquancy, unexpected little shivers

and punch lines. It ended with a slightly

jerky procession of marionettes. Their movie

will take us to a wax museum where we'll hear

a terrible howling, and witness the hammering

of wax fists against the walls of a plywood

diorama. It will be called *The Poet's Dream*.

I'll be watching it in a theater from which

there will be, of course, no exit.

Maybe you'll tell them someday

about the night of intoxicated
dogs about the danger of self-
immolation in the fire of some
idea about the time the world
opened up for us when it
cleaved to its innermost quick
and everything around us seemed
miraculous and good they should
know how to arrange their faces
into masks of splendid inaccessibility
they should know about that certain
windblown nothingness of days
we used to call *our autumn nirvana*
they should know that their mother's
mother was shattered by suffering
and that her mouth remains
forever open in a final cry that

beneath the weight of our own
foretold extinction in the most
intimate corner of every night we
hallucinate inside our bodies'
blood each of these dreams revealing
something dawn's guillotine will
sever from us in the vapid morning
that this is why so many of us walk
around with our eyes stunned . . .
exploding inside as if our brains were
full of infuriated atoms.

Please take me to another world, I'd said

Bizarrely frozen in front of an idle day, I
wonder what there ever could have been to
write about. I am ashamed of my nakedness,
of being alive, of having uttered anything.
So I trace the migration of microscopic spiders
across my living room. I worry about the baby
crying in the window of the apartment next door.
I fear that the local crows are possessed by
shamans. I try to imagine angels pissing
anywhere. Finally, in desperation, I write:
Never cooperate with the Inquisitors! and:
Sky the color of sad wool! All around me, oak
trees shiver in bright sun as if their leaves each
held a little mirror. Points of light dart magically
around my yard. It seems for a moment as if I'm
living in the center of a diamond. Which frees me,
briefly, from the prison of first-person narration.

Memories cut short by the glimmer of a single idea

There was that evening
with silver palm fronds

and that smoke-dried
afternoon after the canyon

burned A night at home
when we held each other

without suspicion God
then that summer when each

day rose like a bubble dripping
ethereal iridescence That

philosopher or madman
we met at our cafe saying *At*

the rim of the gap between memory
and fact all language evaporates

Me saying does it

Something is dancing in the corner of my eye

for Marlena Dalí

When the ship came chugging into harbor, its
smokestacks emptying right into our mouths—you

didn't budge. You didn't budge even when the
flames painted on my shirt reached higher and higher.

Even when a bear head appeared at the end of my
left wrist, snarling. And now this figure dancing

in the corner of my eye: is it one of those wild
old ghosts? Whatever it is, it's causing a

commotion in my soul, a lot like the commotion
you created there. You, who were so beautiful

and so small that sometimes you curled up and
slept deep inside my forehead. You were so small

you could straddle my nose and hug my face. *Tiny*
Dancer, I sang to you while writing the briefest, most

discreet poems to keep you breathing—poems with
tiny clawfoot tubs and miniature cellos. Please

understand I'm light years older now than I used
to be, despite the cosmetics. You say I shed antlers

in the left ventricle of your heart—and that all your
hopes began as glimmers in the corners of my eyes.

When I try to capture what's been dancing there,
what I find are traces of the original rainbow.

Everything matters, but nothing matters for long

What matters. Well, there's the cheapness, the
shoddiness, the tawdriness of the material world

which sings to me of the decay inherent
in all things. Also, silvery flakes of sky and

the red curtains that hang swollen with still air
in my womb-like studio. That moment

in "Blood on the Tracks" where Dylan
says "little red wagon" and it sounds

like "lurid wagon." Days when
the beauty of the world seems to separate and

ascend and with enormous fragrance enter into
eternity, even though we fear that it doesn't. Some

days all of my poems strike me as rewrites of that
song "My Favorite Things." It's a terrible song

except when it's played by John Coltrane
for like 20 minutes.

I don't want to complain

Nor do I want to drape this moment

in a tragic costume or deck it out in gloomy

ostentation. Look, I've always operated

on a fairly minimal dose of reality—I'm

easily beguiled by the séance's spinning table,

and can often be found wandering among

astral swarms, running a licked finger from

star to star across entire light-years. But

darkness is writing tiny poems on the onion

skin of my arms tonight. As far as I can tell,

there's a little ode to the musicality of tree

limbs, and one to the perpetual midnight of

my eyes. There's a haiku describing those

colorful deliriums with which autumn struggles

as it dies (my translation). I guess that's better

than me writing 'nothing' in several languages

on my forearm, which I was just about to do.

Or not to be

The desire to be nothing: it's a wish
that I, in my absurdity, obsess about.

I bear arms against it with the help
of poetry. Ah, poetry!

Fernando Pessoa said that writing
poetry was

his way of being alone.
I write so that one day one of my poems

might brighten someone's obscure
inner landscape with its perfection.

That's only half a lie. I remember
a graduate poetry

workshop in which the poet/teacher
asked the class

who among us wanted to get a job
at a university, publish poems, live a

comfortable life, and who,
instead, wanted to write one truly

immortal poem before they die.
I was the only student poet who chose

the second option. Yes,
that dumbshit

was me. (*Please,*
if you could, says Pessoa,

a little more wine
because life is nothing.)

A mockingbird whistles
insistently in my yucca.

Why, poet, I imagine it saying,
do you moan your depressing phrases

into the atmosphere? While the wind
in the tree limbs sings

an Aeolian song. While there are
openings in the sky

that will soon enough overflow with
flocks of white birds soaring, or

with bushes full of perfect camellias.
Why does it bother you that,

amid all the ineffectual fluttering
in the mind—what's been,

what's to come, what won't ever be—
amid the suffering and sorrowing—

I'm still singing? Don't you
know that when you

empty yourself of your life,
your life remains?

What happens when you empty
yourself of your death, I wonder.

Ah, poetry.

The Art of Poetry

The only thing I traffic in is language.
But once, when I was working on an essay

called "The Era of Writing with Fists,"
I felt a sliver of light from beyond the clouds

start to glow inside me. You'd have
thought the cloud-gods were pulling

my soul up into the sky with a cord of light—
the sky that that day seemed rich, like warm

milk with a pat of butter dissolving in it.
Various thoughts then roamed the grassland

of my mind—thoughts like "I might actually
be happier up there." Thoughts I have failed

to translate into poems with either pencil or
fist. Today in the plaza, I walked past a small

stone statue of a girl reading a book. Each
time I do this I'm afraid that one day she'll

start turning the marble pages, at which point
my own pages will turn to stone. May we never

be slaves who are fed to the lions. May I
spend the rest of my days immersed in the

metaphysics of redemption.

What will save us

I watch my soul plummet
into the green flames of oblivion.

Trying to stop it seems to me to show
a lack of respect for a lifetime of

downward trajectory which
started with a mango margarita.

I'm sure this has been said before:
only the mockingbird is real.

Only a downcast eye can see.
These poems exist where all poems exist—

somewhere between their words
and what they're talking about.

They could save us if we wanted them to.

Notes

The inspiration for "Mockingbird's Proverbs" comes from William Blake's "Proverbs of Hell."

The penultimate sentence in "Proverbs #4" is an adaptation of a sentence in Carlo Rovelli's *White Holes.*

In "Proverbs #6," the poem references the book *I Have More Souls Than One* by Fernando Pessoa.

The penultimate sentence in "Proverbs #7" is a quote from Marcel Proust's *In Search of Lost Time.*

The last lines of "Proverbs #12" allude to Wallace Stevens' poem "Anecdote of the Jar."

The italicized line at the end of "I have become imaginary too" is Lorca's.

The title of the second section of the book "A Portion of Shadow" comes from Antoine Volodine: " . . . a portion of shadow always subsists in the moment of explanation or confession . . . " *Post-Exoticism in 10 Lessons. Lesson 11.*

The poem "The poet at 17" alludes to the Larry Levis poem "The Poet at Seventeen."

The epigraph to "The arbitrary as inevitability" is taken from Yun Wang's *The Book of Mirrors.*

The next to last lines of the poem "Or not to be" quote the last lines of Mark Strand's poem "The Remains." The near quotes of Fernando Pessoa are taken, again, from *I Have More Souls Than One.*

Acknowledgments

"The moon is in labor" was published as a Poem-a-Day by the Academy of American Poets.

"Elegy for all of us" was published in *Nimrod International Journal.*

"Both of my hands are frightened" and "I'm no longer eager for danger" were published in *Agni*.

"A friend asked me about my childhood" was published in *Catamaran;*

"Let the complicated times roll" and "We sit as if in a birdcage, delicately" were published in *Anacapa Review*.

"Your brain is made of glass" was published in *Ilanot Review.*

″I have become imaginary too″ was published in *Volt.*

"They're making a movie of my movie, or you just can't control these things" was published the anthology *Poetry Goes to the Movies*.

"What's that noise?" "The moon is in labor," and "The arbitrary as inevitability" were published in earlier forms in the chapbook *Some Disenfranchised Evening* (Swan Scythe Press).

"This isn't death; it's a hair salon" was published in *The Power of the Feminine I* poetry anthology.

"I have become imaginary too," "Please, take me to another world, I said," and "Memories cut short by the glimmer of a single idea" were published in the anthology *Poetry of Place*.

"The Art of Poetry" was published by *Konkursbuch* in a German translation by Tsveta Sofronieva.

I'd like to thank the editors of the aforementioned journals and anthologies.

Many thanks, too, to my beloved friends and family, to my brilliant workshop poets, to White Pine Press publisher and wonderful poet Dennis Maloney, to the artistry of designer Elaine LaMattina, to my partner, Chuck Rosenthal. All of you contribute an abundance of beauty, truth, and love to my life.

Many of these poems originally appeared as Instagram posts @poetwronsky.

Gail Wronsky's previous books include *Born in a Barn on Venus* (Walton Well Press), a collection of ekphrastic poems with drawings by renowned artist Gronk Nicandro. A chapbook of poems called *Some Disenfranchised Evening,* winner of the Swan Scythe Chapbook Prize, was published in 2024. Other books include *The Stranger You Are*, also with artwork by artist Gronk (Tía Chucha Press), *Dying for Beauty* (Copper Canyon) and *Under the Capsized Boat We Fly: New & Selected Poems* (White Pine Press). The recipient of an Artists Fellowship from the California Arts Council, and a finalist for the Western States Arts Federation Poetry Prize, Gail and her partner Chuck Rosenthal are the founders of What Books Press and Giant Claw, two publishing houses dedicated to discovering and publishing new literary prose and poetry. She lives in Topanga, CA.

Author photo: Alexis Rhone Fancher